Vanishing Lung Syndrome

Miroslav Holub was born in 1923 in Plzeň, western Bohemia, the only child of a lawyer and a high school teacher of French and German. He attended a gymnasium specializing in Latin and Greek, so that Homer and Virgil were the first poets he read carefully. He was brought up to admire Goethe and Romain Rolland and French poetry in general. After graduation in 1942 he was a labourer at the Plzeň railway station. When the war was over, he studied science and medicine at Charles University, Prague, and worked in the department of philosophy and the history of science, and also in a psychiatric ward. He became an MD in 1953 but thereafter specialized in pathology. In his student years he started to write poetry, and became an editor of the scientific magazine, *Vesmir*, the equivalent of *New Scientist*. In 1954, he joined the immunological section of the Biological Institute of the Czechoslovakian Academy of Science and obtained his PhD, the same year his first book of poems appeared. He became associated with the literary group Poetry of Everyday. A prolific writer, he produced almost one book a year until 1969. He was widely translated – fortunately, since between 1970 and 1980 he became a non-person and his work was available only in translation. He worked as an immunologist in New York 1965–7 and in Freiburg in 1968. He has published over 140 scientific papers and three monographs – the last, *Immunology of Nude Mice*, in 1989, in Florida. He has written fourteen books of poetry and five collections of prose. *Vanishing Lung Syndrome* was written between 1985 and 1989, before the events in Czechoslovakia in November 1989.

by the same author

prose
THE DIMENSION OF THE PRESENT MOMENT

MIROSLAV HOLUB

Vanishing Lung Syndrome

*Translated by David Young
and Dana Hábová*

faber and faber

LONDON · BOSTON

First published in 1990
by Faber and Faber Limited
3 Queen Square WC1N 3AU

Photoset by Wilmaset Birkenhead Wirral
Printed in England by
Clays Ltd St Ives plc

A CIP record for this book is
available from the British Library

0-571-14339-3

2 4 6 8 10 9 7 5 3

Some of these poems appeared first in the following periodicals: *American Poetry Review, FIELD, New England Review/Bread Loaf Quarterly* and *Ploughshares*.

Contents

Syncope

Symptom

Syndrome

Synapse

Syncope

(Syncope: Episodic interruption
of the stream of consciousness
induced by lack of oxygen
in the brain.)

That year Diderot began to publish his Encyclopaedia, and the first insane asylum was founded in London.

So the counting out began, to separate the sane, who veil themselves in words, from the insane, who rip off feathers from their bodies.

Poets had to learn tightrope-walking.

And to make sure, officious types began to publish instructions on how to be normal.

What Else

What else to do
but with a stick
drive a small dog
out of yourself?

Scruff bristling with fright
he huddles against the wall,
crawls in the domestic zodiac,
limps,
bleeding from the muzzle.

He would eat out of your hand
but that's no use.

What else
is poetry
but killing that small dog
in yourself?

And all around the barking, barking,
the hysterical barking
of cats.

Yoga

All poetry is about
five hundred degrees centigrade.

Poets, though,
differ in combustibility.
Those soaked in spirits
catch fire first.

What would they be without their disease.
The disease is their health.

They burn, straw dummies,
they don't read Nietzsche,
what doesn't kill you
tempers you.

They smoulder.
They sizzle.
And yet, only a bad yogi
burns his feet
on hot coals.

Great Ancestors

At night
their silhouettes are outlined
against the empty sky
like a squadron of Trojan horses.
Their whispers rise from wells
of apparently living water.

But when day breaks
the way an egg cracks
and full-grown men with truncheons are born,
and mothers bleed profoundly,

they turn into butterflies
with cabbage leaves for wings,
to jelly condensed from fog
in fading, babyish outlines,

their barely discernible hands
shake,

they forget to breathe,
and are afraid to speak a single
intelligible word.

Anyway,
we've picked up more genes from viruses
than from them.

They have no strength.
And we must be the strength of those
who have no strength.

Not for Sale

And how much for
the brain of a pocket mouse,
and how much for
the hump of a humpback whale?

A white sale
in a one-price rag shop,
a sale
of Oshkosh blue jeans
and Collected Works
on crinkled paper.

And how much for a soul?

And how much for
a tub of blood
that yields so little amber serum,
so few antibodies
against the red Shylocks?

How much for us
before we became
priceless?

Gardeners

There's been a bumper crop of gardeners this year.
Some, sprouted in greenhouses, were set out in their
beds by the third full moon. Even the late gardeners
have ripened, and having assumed the poses of statues,
they're thrashing out the philosophy of compost. The
long-day gardeners travel from one cats-tail grass to
another and wrangle with demented dogs-tail grass.
They dream about black daisies and blue-red
strawberries. They trim boxwood into the shape of a
unicorn.

Oh yes, they reply to Hamlet, who is passing by,
there's another garden deep underneath this one, and
that is the question. Certainly, they reply to the
gloomy Antigone, ashes from grave-mounds work
wonders for Cyprian magnolias. And you can't leave
our play either, although the fence stops stray dogs of
misfortune from getting in.

A huge inflatable balloon of the sun rocks above the
garden, and its pink glow makes it impossible to see
that even in the egg a tiny artery is bursting and the
yolk is tainted with blood.

Night Calamities

The storm
went crazy in the darkness.
Prison cells opened.

The sentenced innocents
stamp on the jumping tower. The next routine
is the triple-screw dive while
the tiny infantile Decalogue
drowns by a bank where
tunnel waters
thunderously wash away
flowers from a grave.

Our heel caught in the travertine,
we stare into the runaway dark,
but only the permanently invisible ones
can see us.

The prophet Calchas, just off hand,
categorically demands that the already burned
be burned at the stake, while agreeably whining,
not-so-bright laureates
ride the escalator, as
cities burn down and choke beyond the horizon
and the airport holds a register
of historical errors.

And early, at dawn,
in a burning plane, before the explosion,
a little boy walks down the aisle and says –
Are we there yet, Mum?

Parasite

It rises somewhere in the inner dark
like the fruit of a surplus morning star.
It eats with a worm's tiny mouth,
sweetly round, lined with hooklets
of embryonic exactitude.

It grows, releasing one segment after another,
impregnated by the drowsy ballads of mucosae,
embedded in agreement's protective slime,
it grows, swells, expands,

outgrows the body of its host
as a child outgrows its mother,
ingesting and digesting affectionately
the last epics dealing with
the life of the Lord of the Flies,

and now it grows bigger and still bigger,
larger than life-sized,
the original body's inside now,
the host is the parasite's parasite,
breathing out night and mucus
like a leaf breathing oxygen,
condensing dew-drops, agreeably crunching
with a scarcely audible smacking
the stiff reality of tombstones without inscriptions.

It spills out from house to town,
and from town into landscape, releasing articles
agreeing in principle with Vesuvius's eruption,
with the Krebs cycle and the cutting off
of right hands and left ears,
agreeing in principle with mercilessness,
agreeing in principle with evolution,
the laws of which it ignores
because of the principles of parasitology,

it attains a philosophical dimension
in which it's the only form of matter,
in which it's the only proportion of disproportion.

And when it shrinks again
to the size of a sigmoid loop,

in the derelict landscape of tombstones and
    mercilessness
there will be a draught, as in a tunnel,
for years the eruption will die away
and little spores of imbecile agreement
will bore into granite and wait there
like wet dynamite.

Skinning

We make a noose, tie it to the ladder or whatever,
pull the hind legs through and tighten the noose.
We cut the skin all around. It's easy.
  In the beginning the fact created the Word.
  And the Word hovered above the abyss.
  Then go your ways and I will be in your mouth
  and I will teach you what you should say.
And now we start skinning: we cut under the loins,
pull the skin over the genitals, tug it down
until the bony tail slips out
like the leg of a crab from the eighth millennium
when talk will no longer be necessary.

With both hands we grasp the bloody, sticky stuff
and pull it down towards the head with all our
  strength,
as if it were a straitjacket
for the fools of god,
revealing the silver nude,
the nymph from Lethe, haemorrhaging
in the muscles and fascias,
we pull it down towards the head
  and don't have to believe a thing because
meaning is lost with the connective tissue.
If necessary, we finish the cutting with a sharp knife
where words are joined too closely to the flesh,
and the skin slips down, we cut around the forelegs
push the joints through and break off

the paws, crack crack the first word, crack the last
    word,
from here up to the morning star, a rustling
of satin can be heard, as if
a blue sky was being torn into strips.

There's nothing in the mind that wasn't
in the senses, and the subcutaneous tissue gives off
a mild stench, like distant smouldering cities.
Thus, working in silence we reach the head.
    And it's easy.
We stop at the neck, slip the fascia
along the jaw, sever the ears and pull them
over the head along with the whiskers, like a winter
    cap
dripping with lymph. Only a muscle
still twitches here and there.

On a framework of laths we stretch the skin
into the approximate shape of the body
and its semantics, the skin like
a pennant dotted with ruptured blood vessels
— the coat-of-arms of the last rabbit
on a blue field.

And the butcher is taught what he should say.

Already the first skinned rabbit
starts running on broken-boned limbs,
romping through fields and green pastures
that refresh him,
already hundreds of empty grey skins,

white scuts showing, run off to the black forests,
and thousands of naked bloody zombies
run into city streets
in mindless oblivion,
    meaningless, but
    deeply engaged in the meaningless,

skin here, bodies there,

yes Andrei, I am Goya, but
how do rotting rabbits concern Goya,
and what are empty skins to Spain,

this is the world of skins
and this the alternative world
of dripping muscles on bone, because
– we feel, with the butcher under the tongue –
the skinning is what matters here,
and it's so easy, Allen,
a skinned Moloch is even more
like a Moloch.

Keeping cool is the main thing.

The countryside with yellow flowers along the brook
where the flocks of empty grey skins
of little rabbits graze,
empty grey fur coats, twitching
their comical little skin noses,
empty skins communicating
by touching whiskers
with Diderot.

The royal capital, with gothic arcades,
where the naked rabbit bodies crowd together
under the lash of the pied pipers, bodies
raped by bodies, nakedness raped
by nakedness, in droll
hectic movements,

the Spanish gabble of the word
stripped of fact,
the drain of fact, left behind
by the word,
an empty Ferris wheel
swooping across the abyss
and towards the zenith.

And it all started
with a mere noose
and a ladder,
or whatever,
to heaven.

Symptom

(Symptom: A sign of physical or
mental disturbance leading usually
to a patient's complaint.)

La Brea

In the tar pits
through the ages
writhe the bones
of sixteen hundred wolves,
twenty mastodons
and one Indian girl
somebody killed
and tossed into
the black bubble of time.

Hence the presence
in history's fluid magnet
of death's head-splitting itch,
teeth falling out,
astounded mastodon trunks,

and birdsong

from the day
she waded through grass,
not knowing what lay ahead.

Skeletons

Those who were greening,
they shall be turned to snow.
Those who were about to fly
shall fall asleep in the tar pits
      like the wolves of La Brea.
Those who called out
shall be turned to an exclamation point
      at the end of a declaratory sentence
      never spoken.
Those who caressed
shall be pierced by a thorn.

So that the snow may find
      a few thousand bytes.
So that asphalt may bear moss
      with a little lamb in every
      fruit-holder.
So that silence may creak a little,
so that thorns may be sorry.

Francisco Pizarro,
who had the heads of the defeated
displayed on sticks
on the Plaza de Armas,
June twenty-sixth, 1541,
wounded by axes and swords,
lamed and bleeding to death,
was saved from decapitation

by hasty burial, in a white gown
with the red cross of St James;

was, in the event,
after a hundred and twenty years,
divided: his skull in a lead box,
his bones mixed with children's bones
in a wooden coffin
and walled in a cellar,
while in the cathedral
for three hundred years
another mummy was displayed
under his name.

Those who won
shall be lost to memory.

In order that everything
can happen once again.

Fish

The Emperor Qin Shi-Huang-ti,
first supreme ruler of China,
reigned for nine months posthumously,
embalmed and seated
on his throne, surrounded
by piles of fish,
just in case
he might smell:

Blind eyes of fish, indulgent
moons of historiography,
fish-spawn, vowels
of the official loyalty oath,

swim-bladders of fish, shrines
of the true faith,
bloody fish-fins, ballots
voting to bury philosophers
alive,

naked little fish skulls, ritual
whispered chants of consent
to the stoning of those
who remember too much,

dried mucus of scales, zeal
of the ladies-in-waiting when Qin
merely rehearsed his immortality
in one of his twenty identical palaces,

fish-gills, safe conducts
good for all time,
fish-guts, the bitter
secrets of the state
where, in any case, sometimes
the emperor gets bumped off,

fish with a round ban against laughter
on their lips, fish, caryatids
with flesh falling off the bones,
fish, phosphorescent catalysts
of eternity,
fish, geniuses of muteness,

cartilaginous fish, bony fish,
little fish, big fish,
imperial fish
with the single distinctive function
of stinking clear up to here.

Funerals

Chekhov's body
was shipped
from Badeweiler to Moscow
in a railroad car
that said, in large letters,
FOR OYSTERS.

Gorky didn't conceal his indignation.

He went to the funeral with Chaliapin –
they joined a procession
with a military band.
It was the funeral of General Keller
killed in Manchuria.

Gorky didn't conceal his chagrin at the mistake.

But what's so bad about oysters?

Poets kept on ice
(swimming in their liquor
and bordered by lemon wedges),
extracted from the shell
(parsley, garlic, oil, thyme; grill),

yes, why such a fuss,

cherry orchards of the General Staff,
seagulls of subordination,
gloomy comedies of epaulettes,
bass voices of infantry bears —

only in later years, it turned out,
did Gorky learn
to conceal his feelings a little.

From the Travels of Abigdor Karo*

That land
is marked by
a multitude of crosses,
large and small,
at crossroads,
along highways,
on a stone or on a tree,
in the far corners
of forests,
and minds,
and towns.

Jesus Christ
is on many of them.
Many are
still free.

*Karo was a sixteenth-century Jewish poet,
the first historical personality buried
in the Prague Jewish Cemetery.

The Steam Car

When Josef Bozek, the inventor,
constructed his steam-driven
car, followed by his
steam-driven 'water boat',
seven yards long,
he organized, 1 June 1817,
a public showing in Stromovka Park
for the high nobility
and the enlightened public
upon payment of an entrance fee.

Things had no sooner begun
than there was a sudden downpour
and in the resulting confusion
somebody stole the cash box
and the proceeds.

So that Bozek, the inventor,
lost all his money.

He demolished the steam car
with a sledgehammer.

Since that time
no steam-driven conveyances
have been seen in Bohemia.

The downpours
come frequently.

Glass

Li Po was glass.
Kant was glass.

We observe ourselves like transparent
sea anemones.
We see the dark purple heart
beating,
we see the grey lungs, wings
rising and falling,
we see the oligochaetic
worms of thought
gnawing under the cap.

Linnaeus was glass.
Mozart was glass.
Franz Josef was glass.

In the transparent belly
we see the tubular moon,
and behind the crystalline mouth
the swallowed words.

A prisoner is glass,
a policeman is glass,
sixty glass robots
reside in the castle.

Behind the swallowed words
we see the glass-wool
of incessant melody.

Only the dead
draw the curtain
from within.

The Pedestrian: Lower West Side, New York

At six thirty every night
he walks down Bleecker Street
stopping to look at a print
in a shop window: The Last Judgement.

At six thirty-eight he crosses
Bedford Street, going towards
St Luke's, stops at the corner
to stare intently
at rush-hour traffic.

Then he slips into Wendy's
and points to a Coke, but
they won't let him have it,
every day, no day.

At six fifty he falls to his knees
at the corner of Hudson and Clarkson
in front of the sidewalk signboard
for Spicer's Pet Shop
(Dogs, Cats, Aquarium Accessories).

For twenty minutes,
hands crossed on his chest,
he prays, either to Spicer,
or to the dogs,
or to the cats,
or to the fish,
or to New York,

or to the giant mouse of darkness
which has ten thousand eyes
in twenty-eight floors.

At seven fifteen,
soul purified,
he returns to his hotel,
where blue roses bloom on the walls
like blows from fists,
and Ra, the Egyptian god,
wearing the head of a jackal,
stares down from overhead.

Haemophilia/Los Angeles

And so it circulates
from the San Bernardino Freeway
to the Santa Monica Freeway and
down to the San Diego Freeway and
up to the Golden State Freeway,

and so it circulates
in the vessels of the marine creature,
transparent creature,
unbelievable creature in the light
of the southern moon
like the footprint
of the last foot in the world,

and so it circulates
as if there were no other music
except Perpetual Motion,
as if there were no conductor
directing an orchestra of black angels
without a full score:

out of the grand piano floats
a pink C-sharp in the upper octave,
out of the violin
blood may trickle at any time,
and in the joints of the trombone
there swells a fear of the tiniest staccato,

as if there were no Dante
in a wheelchair,
holding a ball of cotton to his mouth,
afraid to speak a line
lest he perforate the meaning,

as if there were no genes
except the gene for defects
and emergency telephone calls,

and so it circulates
with the full, velvet hum of the disease,
circulates all hours of the day,
circulates all hours of the night
to the praise of non-clotting,

each blood cell carrying
four molecules of hope
that it might all be something
totally different
from what it is.

They Asked the Gods

The Aztecs
asked the gods
every fifty-two
years
if they could go on
living.

>   We did not come to the Earth to stay for ever.
>   Yiao yiao ayiao Ohuaya.

During
the Nemontemi,
the five days
of destruction,
they put out their fires,
demolished households,
ate nothing,
screeched.

>   Here in the middle of the plain,
>   I long for death on the edge of obsidian.

Pregnant women
turned into pigs,
children into rats
and muskrats.

>   Above Jaguar's dogs-tail grass, Eagle is crying.
>   The landscape of mists is coloured red by smoke.

The priests
on top of the volcano
waited to see whether
Aldebaran
would rise
to the centre
of the sky.

It did.

They made a new fire
in the chest
of a fresh human sacrifice
whose heart they had torn out,
runners carried out
Fire-New-Life
by torches
to all the altars,
to all the towns,
to all the families.

Thousands of prisoners
were sacrificed
with cheers
for another cycle
in the life
of the Aztecs.

They began to rebuild,
obsidian was split,
jaguars were born,
and eagles too,
but

We did not come to the Earth to stay for ever.

Until the plumed serpent
Quetzalcoatl
burned himself on the shore,
and in his place
Hernando Cortés
and his metal men
emerged from the sea
and took matters in hand,
including that Aldebaran
and the navel of heaven.

Here in the middle of the plain,
Above Jaguar's dogs-tail grass, Eagle is crying.

And the Aztecs, in fact,
had nothing left
to ask about.

And what do *we* have to ask about?
Yiao yiao ayiao Ohuaya.

Nineveh

Clay tablets wail:
These are bad times, the gods are mad,
children misbehave and
everybody wants to write a book.

Why don't minstrels
go from house to house
howling their bull-like songs
the way they used to?

Have they succumbed to flat-headedness
and frog laryngitis?

Wheezing minstrels engrave the tablets,
libraries no one will ever penetrate
grow wild,
and in their midst
Nineveh's dying.

A Small Town in the Sonora Desert

Walkmen on their ears,
saguaros come down the mountains,
too many walkmen.

The mucous membrane of civilization
grows rampant on every corner:
too many menstruations
and a single pregnancy.
Moreover, the immature fetus
had a mouse
in the fourth brain ventricle.
It happened at night,
when with walkmen on their ears,
saguaros came down the mountains.

Too many saguaros:
in the morning we admitted everything
except ourselves.

Syndrome

(Syndrome: A group of symptoms and objective signs characterizing a disease or a defect of a structure or function.)

Parallels Syndrome

Two parallels
always meet
when we draw them ourselves.

The question is,
ahead
or behind us.

Whether the train in the distance
is coming
or going.

Incense Syndrome

We burned the Christmas incense
so that the Christmas bread would feel like crooning.

We tied ribbons
to ensure the return of miraculous white earthworms.
We listened to nocturnal voices
in our porcelain cave.

But there were only
the digitalized dead. There were only
arthropods craving the moist morphology
of the doughs.
Even those voices knew nothing better
than incense.

In any case it smelled good.
Though one of the kids got a headache.

Wenceslas Square Syndrome*

December.
Eleven o'clock at night,
gilded by sodium light, the smog of silence
hugging the ground. The bronze eye of the horseback
    prince
follows the foot-patrol. Here and there a silhouette
    passes,
rather unreal.

But from the linden that forgot
to lose its leaves resounds a blackbird's mighty voice,
the song rises and drops into the subway,
song of the only December schizophrenic blackbird,
mighty, everlasting song of the only
schizophrenic blackbird,
yes, of course,
a song.

*1988.

The Stiff Man Syndrome*

A gigantic aeroplane
stands in the air, tail down,
above the city,
too heavy
to really take off,

like a fertilized dragonfly,
with its hidden ovipositor
leaving its dead on the rooftops.

We ignore what's up. We stiffen
in muscular spasms,
turning to statues from the waist up,
unable to turn the head
five degrees to the right or left,

after the manner of statesmen,
secretly amazed by the city
which is collapsing in its effort
to wake up.

*Moersch—Woltman.

Kuru, or the Smiling Death Syndrome

We aren't the Fores of New Guinea,
we don't indulge in ritual cannibalism,
we don't harbour the slow virus that
causes degeneration
of the brain and spinal cord with spasms, shivers,
progressive dementia and
the typical grimace.

We just smile,
embarrassed, we smile,
embarrassed, we smile,
embarrassed, we smile.

Vanishing Lung Syndrome*

Once in a while somebody fights for breath.
He stops, getting in everyone's way.
The crowd flows around, muttering
about the flow of crowds,
but he just fights for breath.

Inside there may be growing
a sea monster within a sea monster,
a black, talking bird,
a raven Nevermore that
can't find a bust of Athena
to perch on and so just grows
like a bullous emphysema with cyst development,
fibrous masses and lung hypertension.

Inside there may be growing
a huge muteness of fairy tales,
the wood-block baby that gobbles up everything,
father, mother, flock of sheep,
dead-end road among fields,
screeching wagon and horse,
I've eaten them all and now I'll eat you,
while scintigraphy shows
a disappearance of perfusion, and angiography
shows remnants of arterial branches
without the capillary phase.

*Burke.

Inside there may be growing
an abandoned room,
bare walls, pale squares where pictures hung,
a disconnected phone,
feathers settling on the floor
the encyclopaedists have moved out and
Dostoevsky never found the place,

lost in the landscape
where only surgeons
write poems.

Crush Syndrome*

Once when, in winter dark,
I was cleaning the concrete-mixer,
its cogwheels, like the teeth
of a bored rat of Ibadan,
snapped up the glove
with the hand inside. The finger bones
said a few things you don't hear very often
and then it grew quiet, because
even the rat had panicked.

In that moment
I realized I had a soul.
It was soft, with red stripes,
and it wanted to be wrapped in gauze.

I put it beside me on the seat
and steered with the healthy hand. At the clinic,
during the injections of local anaesthetic
and the stitching,
the soul held firmly with its mandibles
to the stainless-steel knob of the adjustable table.
It was now whitish crystal
and had a grasshopper's head.

The fingers healed.
The soul turned, at first,
to granulation tissue,
and later a scar, scarcely visible.

*Bywaters.

Job's Syndrome

The body no longer recognized itself.
From their nests in the skin
little vampires with fluorescent eyes
flew out.

Disease like a slug with exposed gills.
Disease like a menhir erected
out of horizontal white insomnia.

In the black depths of principle
under all the scabs
even Job is still
a little bit glad to be alive,

out of touch.

Diagnoses

Measles provoke
    the onset of evening, like heavy felt.
Cavities in the teeth
    open rocks.
Smallpox pits
    give contours to the map.
Radiation diseases
    show us our place in the cosmos.
Liver inflammations increase
    Fragonard's sensitivity to ochres.
Cardiac apoplexies
    change the outcome of battles
    in bronze reliefs.

When you're mad as hell,
    it's the general adaptation syndrome.
When you feel like a vegetable,
    you must have been forgotten in a herbarium
    by vegetarians.

Animal Rights

Pity for dogs
          that cry
(boundless pity).
Pity for mice
          that squirm.

Pity for earthworms
          that wither helplessly
(limited pity).
(Pity for protozoons
          that sway their cilia
          so desperately.
Pity for cells
          that crawl away
          for life).

Pity for the central nervous system,
          microglia excepted.

Patients
with progressive amyotrophic lateral sclerosis
can just fuck off. They shouldn't have been born.
Hieronymus Bosch be with them
for ever and ever amen.

The Festival

At the festival of the patients
with all the known diseases
the crutch choir sings
for the pacemakers.

The double astigmatic landscape
gratefully swallows the murmurs
of the mitral valve.

In the candlelit college hall
corticosteroids anoint psoriases.

In the pavilion of intensive care
fish with fish skin disease
are given artificial respiration.

But in fact
we bubble with joy
like fish in a fish tank,
with green joy,

that all this torment
at least has a name.

Synapse

(Synapse: 1. The region of
communication between two
neurons. 2. The linkage between
parental chromosomes preserving
their individual identities.)

Heart Transplant

After an hour

there's an abyss in the chest
created by the missing heart
like a model landscape
where humans have grown extinct.

The drums of extracorporeal circulation
introduce
an inaudible
New World Symphony.

It's like falling from an aeroplane, the air growing
    cooler and cooler,
until it condenses in the inevitable moonlight,
the clouds coming closer, below the left foot, below
    the right foot,
a microscopic landscape with roads like capillaries
pulsing in counter-movements,
feeble hands grasping for the King of Blood,
'Seek the Lord while he may be found,'
ears ringing with the whistles of some kind of cosmic
    marmots,
an indifferent bat's membrane spreading between the
    nerves,
'It is unworthy of great hearts to broadcast their own
    confusion.'

It's like falling from an aeroplane
before the masked face of a creator
who's dressed in a scrub suit
and latex gloves.

Now they are bringing, bedded in melting ice,
the new heart,
like some trophy
from the Eightieth Olympiad of Calamities.

Atrium is sewn to atrium,
aorta to aorta,
three hours of eternity
coming and going.

And when the heart begins to beat
and the curves jump
like synthetic sheep
on the green screen,
it's like a model of a battlefield
where Life and Spirit
have been fighting

and both have won.

The Cloud Shepherd of Hans Arp

Born by Caesarean section,
(while others were thrown out into the world
with the bath water), left out of
anthologies resembling
ovens for Christmas cookies,

with eye fundi unaffected
by doleful poetic diabetes,

he minds a unicorn on meadows
towelled by unexpected frost
for local anaesthesia,

and watches the way churches
trickle out of towns,
one after the other,
and wander through Jutland fields,
gathering like sheep,
heads together,

how streetcars leave towns
in red flocks,
and bury themselves like
buzzing burying beetles
in winter molehills,

watches how traffickers march out of towns,
like lemmings heading for a far away sea,

and he notes that all that is left of towns
is a wall with children's stick-figure drawings

and a big, raised
aluminium parabola,
shining in the sun,
like pharaoh's sword, though
with a jingle-bell at the end,
and rising towards a sky upholstered
with the silk of cosmic probes,

and
(while others make compost
of poetry to grow forget-me-nots
and Chinese cabbage), he inadvertently
plants a thin and tender
line by Hans Arp,

he is smiling
because he knows about the coming
disintegration of towns
and the birth of a new geometry.

Landscape with Poets

Some day when
everything's at rest,
in the curly landscape painted by Rubens
as a background for Baucis and Philemon,

poets will disperse,
in dark capes and hoods,
mute as the silhouettes of milestones,
at five-hundred-yard intervals to the horizon and
   beyond,

and in succession
will strum their electric guitars
and say their verse, strophe, poem,
like a telegram from one stone to another,

in succession,
like automatic keys
on a pipe organ
fingered by monsoon rains,

solitary trees will
hum boskily, sheep
will raise shaggy heads,
Orpheus underground will sound
the upper harmonic registers

and the words will float like clouds,
across the information threshold,
up to the shallow sky,
like proteinoids and oligonucleotides,
words as honest as chemical bonds,
words with the autocatalytic function,
genomic and decoding words,

and there will be
either a new form of life
or, possibly,
nothing.

Piety

They always
            put the flowers right into a vase
the vase into the hall, in a dark cool place
to make the bouquet last.

They died.
            The little urns with their ashes stand
in the hall, in a dark cool place,
and a blind spider
looks after them, so that . . .

Otherwise all this
would be too sad.

The Sun of Hope

They'll certainly remember,
in the twenty-third century
they'll certainly gratefully remember,

preserved
in liquid nitrogen,
implanted in a uterus,
forty per cent of them
revivable,

they'll certainly remember
over the futuristic earth-smoke
and St John's wort,
in the focal point of xenon suns,

they will remember themselves,
actual calves.

The Clock

In the tenth century
a monk named Gilbert
put together the first
mechanical clock:
the human spirit's yearning
towards the Eternal Infinite
needed to be marked off
by a regular sound.
It needed a balance wheel,
an acrobat hanging on a bar
coming loose.

The regular sound begot bells
the synchronized bells
begot towns,
the towns begot cities, the cities begot more hours,
the hours begot
minutes,
the minutes begot
seconds,
a second begot a moment.

And there is no nature in a moment.
No town. No bells, no tick.
No monk. No ash.

The acrobat in the cupola
reaches for a bar
which isn't there.

Spacetime

When I grow up and you get small,
then –

(In Kaluza's theory the fifth dimension
is represented as a circle
associated with every point
in spacetime)

– then when I die, I'll never be alive again?
            Never.
Never never?
            Never never.
Yes, but never never never?
            No . . . not never never never,
            just never never.

So we made
a small family contribution
to the quantum problem of eleven-dimensional
   supergravity.

Formula One

They still don't know all the words for crosswords,
and participles are still
foreign to them. From all
their Easter eggs hatch
twittering Formula One racing cars,
that start at the dog's hair
and finish at the blessed
dried-up earthworm
to the cheers of ants.

They still own the keys
to the Big Bang.

Even if some day they grow up to be
Dante,
or Andretti,
or Feynman,

it will never be as good again.

It will be,
at best,
a fish bowl, with the bubbling
of fish enjoying their muteness.

The Fall from the Green Frog

Yes, little boy, you were drowning a bit.
You toppled off the inflatable green frog
into the swimming-pool, and you were drowning
   agreeably, as if you wanted
once more to see the world from down there, from the
   side
of Moorish flutes and black princesses.
The little head kept bobbing up and disappearing
like a curious seal,

like the torso of a visionary who crashes through
the firmament, beholding the signs
of Virgo and Aries, and a coiffed lock
of God's hair, while the shepherd's staff
drops to earth in superfluous amazement.

Your little voice dissolved in the blue-green,
and your tiny talk shivered
ashore, abandoned. And already on the horizon,
behind the trees, the small skull of the evil new moon
   was rising,
when we dragged you out and comforted you,
while your newly found, bitter-milky
bellowing carried to the suns.

Yes, little boy. And you see, in a way,
this is how you get initiated into life. It's always
a spot of trouble and some unwrapped confusion.

Half-choked by the rush of moments and the rush of
    molecules,
we gasp for breath and climb on to the vault
of the universe, which is no bigger than the frog,
than the stage of the world's smallest theatre.

And we always find that the main button
is missing, or there's a stain on the jacket, or
we forget our lines, or the word forgets us,
it's always something like a premature birth
with dripping blood, we never have a handkerchief
or an ID card on us, we always get out
of the wrong side of bed, no matter which side it is.
And gangs of flat-headed newts laugh at us,
boletus, king of the mushrooms, is splitting his sides.

Mother and Father look meaningfully
at each other, so it's starting for him,
but for us it ends, because Mother
drowned in her lung edema ten minutes ago,
she looks alive, but the rattle is over. And Father
was cremated with a ribbon of vomit in the corner
of his mouth.

So you're all alone, little boy,
you haven't learned your part yet, and there's no one
to prompt. And to comfort.
And yet, you'll often go
underwater, into the blue-green, into the signs
of Virgo, Aries and Trouble, so very
tangible in the pregnant belly of time.

Resembling all the partly born
with the head of a seal, surprised
in superfluous amazement, stiff
before performing in the world's smallest theatre,
under the always malign new moon
on the back of the inflatable green frog.